WHO MOVED MY JOB?

WHO MOVED MY JOB?

Mark Kobayashi-Hillary

Viva Books

New Delhi | Mumbai | Chennai | Kolkata | Bangalore | Hyderabad | Kochi | Guwahati

First Indian Edition 2009

VIVA BOOKS PRIVATE LIMITED

- 4737/23 Ansari Road, Daryaganj, New Delhi 110 002
  E-mail: vivadelhi@vivagroupindia.net, Tel. 42242200
- Plot No. 76, Service Industries, Shirvane, Sector 1, Nerul, Navi Mumbai 400 706
  E-mail: vivamumbai@vivagroupindia.net, Tel. 27721273, 27721274
- Jamals Fazal Chambers, 26 Greams Road, Chennai 600 006
  E-mail: vivachennai@vivagroupindia.net, Tel. 28290304, 28294241
- B-103, Jindal Towers, 21/1A/3 Darga Road, Kolkata 700 017
  E-mail: vivakolkata@vivagroupindia.net, Tel. 22836381, 22816713
- 7, Sovereign Park Apartments, 56-58, K. R. Road, Basavanagudi, Bangalore 560 004
  E-mail: vivabangalore@vivagroupindia.net, Tel. 26607409, 26607410
- 101-102 Mughal Marc Aptt. 3-4-637 to 641, Narayanguda, Hyderabad 500 029
  E-mail: vivahyderabad@vivagroupindia.net, Tel. 27564481, 27564482
- Beevi Towers, First Floor, SRM Road, Kaloor, Kochi 682 018, Kerala
  E-mail: vivakochi@vivagroupindia.net, Tel: 0484-2403055, 2403056
- H. No. 12, P. B. Road, Near Arya Hospital, Rehabari, Guwahati 781 008
  E-mail: vivaguwahati@vivagroupindia.net, Tel: 0361-2735624

www.vivagroupindia.com

Published by arrangement with

Mark Kobayashi-Hilary
National Outsourcing Association
44 Wardour Street
London W1D 6QZ
United Kingdom

ISBN: 978-81-309-1211-0

Published by Vinod Vasishtha for Viva Books Private Limited,
4737/23, Ansari Road, New Delhi-110 002.

Typeset by Etica Press Ltd., Malvern, Worcs

Printed and bound by Raj Press, R-3, Inderpuri, New Delhi - 110 012.

This book is dedicated to both the old
and the new within my family
My grandfather, John Jenkinson
(1922–2008)
and my nephew Lewis Hillary
(2007–).

John left Ireland seeking work in
England in the 1950s and never went
home. He was a credit to the tradition of
the hard-working Irish migrant.

Sláinte granddad!

Contents

The **Author**

Mark Kobayashi-Hillary is the founder of the international small business exchange Peerpex.com. He is well-known as a British writer and blogger having written several books focused on outsourcing, change, and globalisation including:

- 'Outsourcing to India: The Offshore Advantage' (Springer 2004, 2nd ed. 2005)
- 'Global Services: Moving to a Level Playing Field' (BCS 2007, co-written with Dr Richard Sykes)
- 'Building a Future with BRICs: The Next Decade for Offshoring' (Springer 2007)
- The Outsourcing Yearbook (VNU Incisive 2007)

Mark writes regularly for the British technology journals *Computing* and *silicon.com*. He is a board member of the UK National Outsourcing Association and a founding member of the British Computer Society working party on offshoring.

Mark teaches postgraduate students at the London South Bank University. He founded the corporate blogging service *Blogpistol.com* and he is a director of the peer-to-peer foreign exchange company *fxaworld plc*.

Mark enjoys music and he usually reads fiction more often than management books (sorry). Mark also enjoys walks in London parks with Matilda, his Staffordshire bull terrier.

Mark lives in London, England.

www.markhillary.com

National Outsourcing Association

www.noa.co.uk

Acknowledgements

This book is an experiment in a number of ways for me. First, it is an entirely new form of writing to that I am used to. I had an idea that I could use a short story to illustrate some ideas around career change, migration, and outsourcing. I've written about this subject in my journalism and more academic books, especially 'Global Services', but I always wondered how the debate could be stimulated – not necessarily with all the answers at hand, but at least brought a little more mainstream. I wondered why should I write a long and detailed study when a short story about dogs may well be more effective? A detailed study may be considered more worthy within the confines of academia, but it will hardly encourage public debate.

I will have succeeded in my quest if the topics of offshoring, outsourcing, migration, and lifelong education requirements start to become more intertwined in public debate. They really need to be connected together as people consider the present and future impact of how services are globalising – and how that affects their job. Companies today are structured differently to the past and that affects all of us. The journalistic mirage of 'jobs vanishing to India' still appears every time a major corporation locates a new team or entire office in Asia. Yet the debate is far more complex than the persistent popular newspaper views on cheap labour indicate.

Mature and developed societies need to understand that this century really is going to be different. The endless increase in the global price of oil (and food) is one obvious consequence of rapid development in Asia, particularly China – but there will be more change to come in our lifetime.

This is a lot to convey using a short story about dogs on a farm in England, but I hope the story creates some debate that explores both the value and dangers of migration and offshoring, along with a pragmatic exploration of how better to prepare for a changing world. The general adoption of the Internet in the 1990s has created a global information network that will change how people work forever. This really is a time of industrial revolution, for services of all kinds.

In my 'Global Services' book I had highlighted lulu.com as a publisher of the future. A publisher that can offer books to the regular global book trade, but only printing them as they are needed, even right down to printing a book only when it is sold. I thought I should try to use lulu.com rather than return to a traditional publisher with this book – I have written about the company, so I should try some of my own medicine. If you never see me publish with lulu.com again in future then I guess you can assume the experiment did not work, but I am confident of using this new technology to reach a wide audience.

This book owes a debt of inspiration to two authors, both of whom I admire and I am humbly in their debt. Dr Spencer Johnson published his parable 'Who Moved My Cheese' in 1998 and proved that even in these modern times you can still use allegory to make a point. Before Dr Johnson's success with this book I guess most people assumed that this form of writing had ceased with Aesop, or more recently, the New Testament. I've used a similar title as a nod of respect to what Dr Johnson has achieved with the form. If you have not read his book, then go and buy a copy now. The English writer George Orwell is my other source of inspiration. Orwell was a brilliant novelist –best known for '1984' – but he wrote several book-length non-fiction studies on a range of subjects including working class poverty and the Spanish civil war. When he published 'Animal Farm' in 1945 he demonstrated that a short story could satirise Soviet totalitarianism without literal condemnation. Again, do buy it if you have not read it and for a longer exploration of how Orwell viewed the troubles of a modern society, get a copy of his novel 'Keep the Aspidistra Flying.'

I'm grateful to both these authors for providing the ideas and inspiration for this book. It really is an experiment for me and I entered this project with some trepidation, as many of my friends could not see how this short story might be relevant to them. My answer is that regardless of the story these issues are desperately important and need to be openly discussed. If you have a job today or you are planning to seek a job tomorrow, in any country, then the topics raised by this story are important to you.

I'd like to thank a few colleagues, friends, and family for their help while I was producing this book. First, my entire family – I'm hoping that my nephews Luke and Ben can read and understand the story already – Lewis might need a few more years. Matilda, my dog, helped me to relax and think clearly.

Dr Richard Sykes was a great source of ideas and debate, as always.

George Bell and Alan Hovell at London South Bank University allowed me to continue talking to their students.

Kully Dhadda at Flame PR has kept me connected to the media people that matter.

Bryan Glick at Computing and Steve Ranger at silicon.com have both allowed me to continue writing regular journalism and blogs for their journals – as well as silicon.com deputy editor Andy McCue.

My friend John Uncle, and his wife Carol, is an obvious person I should thank profusely for all the canine-related knowledge I have developed since I met him. John has trained dogs all over the world and I'm working now to try capturing some of his memoirs related to dogs and also growing up in London immediately after the war.

The Chief Executive of BT Global Services, François Barrault, has allowed me to do some extensive work with his company this year, which has been extremely interesting. Thanks also to Mark Weeks, Rachael Bell, Caroline Phillips, Ellen Ferrara, Adelise Ashdown and Steve Daly at BT.

My friends Mahesh Ramachandran and Vijay Kumar at fxaWorld plc are showing the world how technology can be used to fight poverty and injustice and I'm proud to be associated with their work.

Martyn Hart, Nigel Roxburgh, and the National Outsourcing Association team along with the great people at Buffalo PR, led by Kerry Hallard, have given me a number of opportunities to explore outsourcing in more detail through their research and events.

I enjoy the good fortune to have a number of friends from all over the world and many of them contributed ideas when I was talking about this project. I'd particularly like to thank Mark Hodges, the founder of Equaterra, for sharing his vast experience with me, Emily Ma and Shiyuan Li for teaching me about China, Analine and Fran for teaching me about Brazil, and Shelley Wilkey for teaching me how Kiwis drink all other nationalities under the table.

My old mates Sean Cook, Kevin Donaldson, and David Leiper deserve a shout. Twenty years ago we were all stacking apples in a Sandhurst supermarket. How times change!

I completed the final draft of this book at a hotel in Vilnius, Lithuania. I'd like to thank my friend Karolina Ayan for recommending I visit such a beautiful city.

I hope you enjoy it. Don't forget to *paws for thought!*

Mark Kobayashi-Hillary

London, September 2008

Chapter One

Winston, Charlie and Blair were all Border Collies working on Manor farm in Bedfordshire, England. They were herding dogs and masters at it, the best sheepdogs you could possibly imagine. There was not a single sheepdog from Cornwall to Kent who could match their skill at rounding up errant sheep. As far as they were concerned, they were the finest sheepdogs in the whole of England.

Sheep are stupid beasts, and it's because of that stupidity that they are so difficult to control. They don't know what to do when they are told. Or they think they know, but they just don't do what they are told. They do sometimes and then they don't. Each sheep follows what the one in front does and so it can be difficult to get those stupid animals to do anything sensible when all they ever do is follow the one in front. They never think ahead one single moment.

Winston, Charlie and Blair hated sheep. How can a real farm animal not be in complete control of its environment? How can a real animal not be concerned about what happens today, tomorrow, or next week? Those moronic sheep would never even think a minute ahead of what they were actually doing – mostly eating - and that's why most of the sheep go to the butcher and the Collies stay on the farm with the humans.

Winston was the oldest of the three sheepdogs at Manor Farm. But even so, none of this herding trio could be really called young anymore. Winston was seven, Charlie was next at six, and Blair was the young pup at four. Maybe Blair could still just about scrape into the human equivalent of the under thirty, but he was pushing it, with a fast approaching fifth birthday. They could not really claim to be spring chickens, but they knew how fit they all were, out every day of the year on the farm working the sheep. They had the lithe bodies and rippled stomach of animals that work to live and live to work.

Winston was always the leader, but the three of them would work as a pack, as a team. There was not a sheep that could escape their combined canine effort. Each morning at about six, the farmer would come out and whistle for the dogs. They lived in the barn that stored the combine harvester and silage. The farmer kept all his really important equipment in that barn and it was right next to the farmhouse. The combine harvester had cost him a fortune; he had borrowed quite heavily to purchase it. All the really important tools and contributors to the farm were right there in that barn. And the dogs lived there too.

Maybe it was because of the dogs, but there were very few rats in that barn. There was never any occasion where they had to go and chase vermin. The rats knew about the dogs and they kept a safe distance. This really was the dog's home. Of course, the rats ate their way through everything they possibly could in every other barn, but in that one the farmer could leave anything he wanted and he knew that it would be fine. They were not even real ratting dogs, like terriers, but the rats were still afraid.

Each morning as dawn broke, the farmer would whistle for his dogs. The Collies would race out to meet him by the farmhouse. Each of the dogs loved the thrill of the first run in the morning and no two days were the same. They would walk and run the short distance from the farmhouse out to the fields, and from there to wherever the farmer planned on working that day.

Sometimes, the farmer wanted to move the entire flock from one part of the farm to another. This was the hardest job of all, yet the three Collies working together could direct and shepherd hundreds of sheep from one field to a gate, and then on to another field. The farmer would call or whistle directions to the dogs, guiding them all the time. He had different commands for each dog so there was never any confusion. Winston always responded to whistles, but the farmer would call out to Charlie in English and in Italian to Blair.

Some jobs were easier. When a sheep was unwell or needed attention for some reason the farmer would only need to point it out, and then they were off. One dog could split a sheep from the pack, but it was more fun doing it together because it upset the sheep. All three of the Collies had a good eye. They could out stare the most stubborn ewe if needed and it was a skill that was called on each day out on the field.

When the Collies finished work in the evening, they would be fed over by the farmhouse. Dinner was usually raw meat and bones with some vegetables too. The farmer would normally leave out chicken wings or lamb chops, but now and again he might add a steak. They all loved venison so it was a huge treat when the farmer left a nice juicy venison steak for them to share.

Winston, Charlie, and Blair had all been born on this farm. They were probably related as cousins somehow, but the farmer had never confirmed it. They behaved like family though, because the farm was all they knew and each one of them had grown up with the other. Winston could recall training Charlie and Charlie could recall training Blair. Winston himself had learned the ropes from another Collie called Derby, who had eventually retired from the fields and lived in the farmhouse for a couple of years before he died. He was buried in the garden by the farmhouse. Winston could recall how the farmers voice was strange for weeks after Derby went – he could hardly whistle or call. The grief was so clear and it only made Winston work harder to prove that he could be as good a Collie as the earlier generation.

The Collies were happy on the farm. Each day they worked hard for their rewards, but they enjoyed the work. It was fun working with the farmer and being an integral part of the team that kept the farm running. They needed the shelter and food that the farmer offered, along with the continued work, but they knew that the farmer needed them more. Without good Collies, a sheep farmer would be lost.

Above all, they enjoyed their work. Working hard made them happy. It made them feel a sense of fulfilment each time the farmer offered praise for a job well done. Each time they woke in the morning they were all ready to work and they loved their life. The farmer had once talked to Winston about dogs in the city and how boring their existence is. No work, no farm, no need to work for food. Some of them sit in a house all day doing nothing, with food supplied twice a day. What kind of a life is that? When Winston had discussed it with the others they all agreed they couldn't live like that. With no purpose or sense of achievement they would all go mad. And some city people even keep Collies like that – cooped up with nothing to herd or chase. The Collies on Manor farm all agreed they were lucky to have the life they have. They were comfortable.

Chapter Two

It was dawn. The piercing whistle of the farmer brought Winston, Charlie, and Blair running from the barn where they liked to sleep. The barn was more comfortable than the farmhouse, even though the farmer would never mind them entering the house. In the barn they had protection from the cold, the sun, fresh water, and just the occasional rat to chase when they were not working – the young rats that had yet to learn about avoiding the dogs.

The farmer was down by the house and he had three dogs there alongside him. They were all sitting in a line looking rather like sentries guarding some historic treasure. These dogs were new on the farm. None of the Collies had ever seen them before.

Winston was perplexed at the strange sight. A sheepdog should only look like a Collie. A Collie can vary in height and weight a little and can be a mixture of black and tan and white, but a Collie is always a Collie. What could the farmer be doing with these strange new animals? They were all clearly dogs, but for certain none of them was a sheepdog.

One had long shaggy hair. It looked a complete mess. His hair was so long it covered his eyes. He kept flicking his head to move the hair away from the front of his face - as if a fly was constantly buzzing around his face. One was quite similar to the Collies, perhaps with a shorter coat, but still quite similar. Certainly dog-like. It was even a similar black and white to the markings of Blair and Charlie's coat. The other dog just looked plain strange. It had a face that was squashed, squashed flat with rolls of skin lolling around his cheeks and chin.

"What kind of dogs are you?" Winston asked. "I don't think I've ever seen a dog like any of you before, especially not around here. Are you here to work with us on the farm? Are you sure you know how to herd sheep?"

The big hairy one responded first, with a warm smile on his face.

"Hello. I'm very pleased to meet you. My name is Lech. I know all about herding sheep, and my friends here do as well. I'm known as a Polish Lowland Sheepdog, or a Nizzy if you prefer. My breed has been herding sheep in Poland for centuries. I'm surprised you have never heard about us – in Poland we know all about the famous Border Collies from Scotland."

"This is England, not Scotland." Winston grumpily retorted. This hairy Polish beast was a bit too good, just too polite, for his own good.

"Yes of course I know that. In fact, I know that this farm is located in Bedfordshire; we are not very far from London, your capital city. An old Border Collie once taught me the history of your breed so I know all about your ancestors on the Scottish borders. You are quite a long way from home as well!" Lech carried on: "Let me introduce you to my friends here. Pandit and Mozi, why don't you introduce yourself to the Collies?"

"Thank you brother." The dog with the squashed face stepped forward a single pace. "Hello. I'm Mozi. I'm a Chinese Shar Pei. We have a proud history stretching back thousands of years as herding dogs and as expert guards to people and their property. The Chinese nobility have valued our protection for longer than China has been known as China. Forget about your tiny highlands in Scotland. Try herding along the Mongolian border and you know what it means to herd dumb animals."

Mozi started scratching his body with a hind leg. The folds of skin on his body sagged and rolled with each scratch. The third dog in the makeshift line grinned and stepped forward a little. He coughed and introduced himself to the Collies.

"I am very pleased to be meeting you. My name is Pandit and I'm known as a Dhangari dog. My own heritage is Indian. To be more precise I originate from a place known as Maharashtra. That's the name of a state in India. You may be aware of Bombay, or Mumbai as it's known now. That's the closest big city to my home. Well, actually Aurangabad is probably the closest big city to my home, but I guess you have never heard of the place. It's very nice – there are some impressive caves nearby. Everyone knows Bombay… sorry Mumbai…"

Lech coughed and interrupted Pandit's flow. It seemed he was used to his Indian friend talking too much and they had an agreed way to end these streams of canine consciousness.

Winston, Charlie, and Blair stared at the dogs – if they could be called dogs - with a sense of disbelief. They were very friendly, but they were not Collies. One had more hair than the sheep he claimed to have experience of herding. All the Collies were thinking the same thoughts without speaking. The sheep must be very strange in Poland. The Shar Pei was so majestic and controlled it appeared as if he could never have really known life on a farm. The Indian dog seemed earnest and hard working and he looks a bit like a Collie, but he sounded very indecisive. Sheep don't let you get away with indecision out in the field. They thrive on it.

Winston wondered out loud: "What is the farmer doing?" Just then, the farmer explained what he was doing.

"I'm glad to see you all getting along with each other. Winston, I'm leaving it up to you to ensure that these new dogs learn about the farm. They need to understand how English sheep behave and how we work around here. Make sure they all feel comfortable on the farm and make sure that all three of them learn everything they need to know. I'm depending on you to do this for me."

So, the new dogs joined the Border Collies on Manor farm. They found another spot within the barn and created their own home there. All six dogs now slept in the barn, but in two groups of three, the English old-timers and the foreign newcomers.

Each morning, when the farmer whistled from the farmhouse, all six dogs would race to be there by his side. Lech, Mozi, and Pandit all had experience of herding sheep, but they found some subtle differences in the way

English sheep behaved. With the expert guidance of Winston, Charlie, and Blair they soon managed to modify their own expertise so it suited the English sheep and the way the farmer liked to manage the sheep.

The farmer could see them improving day by day and he never failed to tell them what a great job they were doing. He never gave such praise to the English dogs, even back when they had been pups learning the ropes. The farmer was even smiling. He had never smiled on the farm before. Winston felt there was something wrong and he called a meeting behind the barn one evening after work, so he could talk privately with Charlie and Blair about the new farm order.

"Something is wrong…" said Winston to the other Border Collies. "Something is seriously wrong. The farmer never explained why he wanted us to train these foreign dogs. We trusted him and believed that there must be some good reason, yet his behaviour is changing, he now appears to favour them before us."

"That's true. I even saw him allowing his children to play with the hairy one." Blair pitched in.

"Look. I've been observing them over the past few weeks" Winston continued. "Have you noticed how their behaviour has changed, especially since they became more confident about the way the English sheep behave? They are always up and out of the barn before us. They go and wait outside the farmhouse, ready for the farmer to come out and start work without calling. They keep on working the herd even after the farmer says it's time to finish and go home for the day. They don't even ask for as much food or bones as the farmer usually leaves for us. In fact, I can't see that they do anything other than trying to please the farmer. They don't even chase the rats at night or howl at the moon!"

Charlie looked worried: "When you say it like that Winston, it makes it sound as if the farmer is replacing us with these foreign dogs. Is that really what you mean?"

"That's exactly what I am concerned about. But I can't quite understand the situation. Surely no farmer would want to run an English farm without English dogs? It doesn't make sense to run a farm here in England with English sheep and to expect foreign dogs to understand how to interact with the sheep."

"But we trained them. We told them everything about the sheep because the farmer told us we should. They can do what we can do now because we trained them!"

Winston looked at Blair and said "Yes Blair, you're right, but even so things are different here. A dog that is born and brought up on a farm in England should be the only dog that can understand the way things are run on an English farm. I don't have any prejudice about other breeds of dog. Some dogs are experts at retrieving, or hunting, or using their nose. We are the best in the world at herding English sheep and so I can't understand why the farmer should have asked us to train these exotic dogs in our methods of herding."

Blair stood up and looked straight at Winston. The younger dog said: "Look, I'm a pretty straight kind of dog. I like the truth to be told and I like to know where I stand, where we all stand. I will go and ask the farmer tomorrow so we know once and for all what is really happening."

Chapter **Three**

But Blair never had the opportunity to ask the farmer because something happened the next morning that changed the life of the three faithful Collies forever.

The Collies all woke late. There had been no whistle that morning. Perhaps the farmer was ill? Perhaps there was some other reason for him to not call the dogs to work today? The foreigners were gone. Charlie looked outside the barn. He could hear the strange bark of the Indian dog Pandit. They were across the farm in the meadow already and working the sheep, but the farmer had not whistled.

The farmer came out of the farmhouse and caught Charlie staring at him. He looked away from the confused dog and walked up the drive to the main farm entrance where he started opening the big wooden gate.

Charlie called the others. All three Collies walked slowly up to the farmer and stood behind him, watching and waiting.

"That'll do, boys." Said the farmer to the dogs without looking at any of the pack. They knew something was wrong because that's what he would normally say at the end of a hard day in the field. Why would he say it at the start of the day after forgetting to call them to work?

A large blue truck turned the corner and entered the farm. The driver stopped the truck in front of the farmer and stepped out. She began talking to the farmer, but most of the words made no sense to any of the Collies, even Winston who was usually able to understand most human conversations.

The driver handed a large piece of pink paper to the farmer, which he signed with a pen, leaning against the side of the truck to support the paper. The driver then took the paper and placed it back inside the cab, before opening the back of the truck. It was empty in there, but arranged into a series of cages on two levels. There were big ones at the bottom and smaller ones up above.

Winston was now getting concerned. He had been examining the blue truck carefully from both sides. He had managed to read the large words painted on the side of the truck:

BATTERSEA DOGS AND CATS HOME
WWW.DOGSHOME.ORG

So the truck was from a dog's home. But when Winston explained this to the other Collies they just asked 'what is a dog's home?' Blair even asked 'isn't the barn our home?' Winston could only nod sagely. He didn't know what was going on either.

The farmer and the truck driver told them to walk into the back of the truck. As each of the Collies passed the farmer he gave the dog a light pat on the head. There were three open cages inside the truck and the Collies assumed they should go into the cages. They didn't need any instruction. It was obvious. The farmer didn't even wait to watch the big blue door being closed. The last Winston saw of the farmer was his back, as he walked slowly to the farmhouse.

When the door closed it was dark inside the truck. It was also quite damp and not very warm. It also smelled because hundreds, or maybe thousands of other dogs had been transported in that truck before and they had all left their mark on it in some way or other.

While the truck was moving Winston explained his thoughts out loud to the other Collies, hoping to reassure them. Winston never usually talked a great deal, but on this journey he felt obliged to keep talking about the different reasons they might be travelling together in the dark in this truck.

"Of course there is bound to be a rational explanation for all this. Either the farmer is sending us away on our first ever holiday, because we now have some effective deputies on the farm, or it is a form of training course. Maybe we are going to learn something new at this dog's home so we can return to the farm soon with our new skills. We might learn how to do even more than just herding, so we can become more useful on the farm."

When the truck stopped and the door opened they found a new place with unusual smells. It was nothing like the farm they had left behind. There was no grass underfoot and the ground here was solid and hard. There were trucks and cars everywhere, hundreds of them passing by one after the other, and the noise was horrendous. Back on the farm the only sound came from the animals, either those on the farm or the wild birds that sung from the trees bordering the fields. Here, there was a deafening cacophony that the three Collies could not understand – it made each one of them uneasy.

Yet they had to venture into this new environment. The human who had driven the truck was friendly, but firm with them. They found themselves led, just like sheep, to a cold new home. It was cold and grey, with a concrete floor. It was a kennel, but it felt more like a prison cell to the three Collies, familiar with the freedom of the English countryside. There were metal bars at the front that allowed humans to watch them. The Collies found that they could no longer run together. They were no longer working. They were trapped inside this concrete box, with the only respite being a walk each morning in the area surrounding the dog's home. Even when they were walked, the humans kept them all chained together on leads, it was not possible to run any longer. The enjoyment they found in each day on the farm had been extinguished.

It could have been worse. At least the humans did keep the Collies together. One morning a group of unfamiliar humans had pointed at Blair. The dog's home staff had removed him from the kennel and started leading him away on a lead. Blair howled for his friends and refused to walk. He forced the humans into dragging him along the concrete by his neck until they gave in. They shook their heads and placed him back in the kennel with Winston and Charlie. Blair watched them leave later that morning with a black Labrador, his tail wagging eagerly.

"Don't worry Blair. I'm sure this is all a mistake. It won't be long before all three of us see the farmer again and are on our way back to Manor farm again. Sometimes it can be impossible to see what is going to happen, unless you watch and wait." Winston was trying to convince himself as much as the other two Collies. None of them really felt that the farmer had made a mistake in abandoning them, but they could not understand why or how it had happened. And it was so sudden. One moment they were highly valued on the farm, an integral part of the way the farmer worked – they were a critical part of the farm team. Then, they were replaced and now they were in a new place they didn't understand and didn't like. Winston's brain ached trying to consider how they might change their new circumstances. He was chewing his paws at night.

During one of the morning exercise sessions Winston ended up on the lead next to an old and wise-looking Staffordshire bull terrier named Matilda. Matilda said she had been in the dog's home for almost a year now because she was eight years old and the humans who came to the home wanted puppies or young dogs, not dogs about to enter their twilight years.

"I feel sorry for you and your friends." Matilda said.

"What do you mean?" Winston replied.

"None of you are young pups. Look at yourselves as a trio; you are just about as old as me and the others are not far off. It's hard enough to get the humans interested in offering a new home to a young dog, but you are old and you all want to stay together as a pack of three. I saw the way Blair behaved when that family offered him a home. That's what will happen to you because it's hard to find homes for Collies in London. You are country dogs and this is the city. You are not really suited to this kind of life, walks in the park, playing with young kids, relaxing on a soft couch. Everyone knows you would rather be chasing sheep and most Collies that end up stuck in city apartments go mad chasing their own tail. You might get lucky and find a family who wants one of you, but there is no way you will ever find someone who wants to offer a new home to three old Collies."

Winston was silent, until he eventually considered that it might be prudent to ask Matilda for advice. After all, she was in a similar position to Winston, Charlie, and Blair and had been there far longer: "If you are right then we might be here a long time, but what do they do to the dogs that can't be placed in a new home? Do we just remain stuck here forever?"

Matilda's smile vanished. Staffordshire bull terriers have the kind of face that makes them look as if they are smiling constantly, but now the smile was gone.

"They give you about a year. Then you just vanish. They take the old dogs in to see the doctor at the back of the home. The old dogs never come back from there. None of us have ever seen a dog return alive from that place. You three have a chance if you split up, but I can't see anyone taking you all together, not here in London. I'm hoping I can find a new owner before my year is up. I wake up each morning hoping that I'm going on one of these walks and not in to see the doctor. I really don't know how much longer they will give me."

The smile returned, but the glint in Matilda's eyes had gone. Winston was worried too. The situation was worse than he imagined. The old life on the farm was gone forever. The three Collies found themselves now useless and unwanted. In a single short journey they had gone from being an essential part of the farm to a dog's home kennel and were now impossible to place with a new family. Winston resolved to keep his pack together. Thanks to Matilda he realised it might be possible to find new homes if they all split up, but they had never known any life other than the life where they supported each other. What possibility would there be of adjusting to a city life if they could not lean on each other for support? It's not possible. "I have to preserve my pack" thought Winston as he paced the city streets, straining on his bright blue lead.

Chapter **Four**

Several months passed in the dog's home. The three Collies were occasionally interrupted in their daily boredom by a human interested in one of them as a potential city pet. It was usually Blair who attracted the most attention. The humans considered that he was the least like a farm dog and the most likely to settle into city life.

"I don't know why the humans all think you are the most attractive," said Charlie one morning after another family with two young children had spent time talking to Blair and petting him. "We all have something to offer a family in the city. I think I could manage to live with a couple of long walks a day, a roaring fire to sleep by and plenty of fresh food whenever I want to eat."

"I'm not trying to attract them. They just like me because I'm the youngest. I guess they think I can be more easily trained to live in a house." Blair had to defend himself from the constant swipes from Charlie.

Winston had to stop them bickering on a daily basis. The arguments were becoming more frequent. Charlie had even taken to sabotaging the chance of Blair finding a friendly home by starting fights whenever a family of humans took an interest in Blair. Each time a child took an interest in Blair, Charlie would nip him until he retaliated. All the humans ever saw was a dog they thought looked happy and friendly suddenly snarling, baring huge teeth and attacking another dog. They always left, often picking their child up from the ground, fearing they might be next in line after Blair finished savaging Charlie.

"This place is a concrete carbuncle and I haven't eaten any natural fresh food for months. What are we going to do Winston? We can't go on here much longer. You know what Matilda said about the dogs that can't find a new home. What's going to happen to us?" said Charlie one day.

Winston could only agree. He could see the life draining from each of his friends, and himself, day by day. They had now been stuck in this home for months with not a single person ever offering a new home. He couldn't decide on a plan though. He didn't know the city and didn't know how to plan a new life away from the home. All three of the Collies were highly skilled at herding. They knew how good they were at controlling sheep, or anything that could be herded. Sometimes the farmer used them to round up the geese, because the geese would wander away from the pond and close to the road. They knew all of this and yet everything they could do was useless in this environment. The Collies herding skills were useless in the city. Could they go around herding cars?

Winston had to accept he was lost. He had no plan of action and no vision that could help the Collies escape to a new home. He often shared his fears with Matilda the Staffordshire bull terrier, but he would always ensure that it was when the other Collies could not listen to their discussion. He respected Matilda's views. She had been born in London. She knew nothing of the countryside and listened respectfully to Winston's stories of life on the farm. Matilda always claimed that she would not know how to live on a farm surrounded by animals. She chased everything, rats and squirrels mainly, but imagine the choices available on a farm full of animals.

Now they were walking through the city streets on a morning walk, on long leads as usual. Another of the dog's home volunteer walkers was walking Charlie and Blair. The walkers were always nice and tried to keep friends together. Matilda and Winston were together as usual.

"I don't think I have much longer." Matilda said quietly to Winston. "The dog's home people keep coming to check on me and they never usually do that. I haven't had any visitors for weeks either. I don't know how much longer they are going to keep me now. I think I might be off to the doctor soon."

Winston was shocked: "What can we do? We can't just let you vanish. You are the wisest dog in the entire home. You know London and you are the only other dog that gives me any hope."

Matilda started talking: "We need to plan an escape. We all need to plan how to escape from this place, but you three need to more than any of the others. Escaping together is not going to be all that hard. They take us out on these walks every day. If we work together, we could easily break free from the walker. What is going to be hard for you is finding what to do after you escape. London is a vast place and there are no farm animals around here. It's a completely different environment unlike anywhere you have ever lived before."

Matilda talked at great length about the differences between the country and the city, about the parks in the city and how fearsome dog wardens often round up the stray dogs found without a human owner. Then she described something that amazed Winston. It was something he could not believe and it made him laugh in amazement.

"I am telling you Winston it's true. I was there and I saw it myself. This was in a park in north London and some local people had set it up to look a bit like a farm. There were fences and pens and barriers. Then all the humans were watching three Border Collies – just like you – guide a small group of sheep around the park and finally into the pen."

"Was there a shepherd or farmer there as well and why would they be doing it in a park? There are no sheep in a park in London. How could it be true?" Winston was perplexed. None of Matilda's story made sense.

"You know what it really was? Entertainment. All these city humans have never seen sheep before. They eat them for dinner, but they've never seen them up close. These humans have never seen the hard work that dogs like you do every day to herd them around a farm. They way I understood it was that the farmer would load up a group of sheep, just six or seven of them, in his trailer. He would drive into the city and set up a pen so it looked just like it would back on the farm. These city folk would pay money just to watch the sheep let loose and the Collies then work to get them back in the pen."

"But that's completely bizarre! It happens every single day on the farm. Why would humans want to pay to watch? They could come to any sheep farm and watch it happening and it wouldn't cost them a thing!"

"Have you ever seen any city folk watching you work on the farm? Has anyone from the city ever been there during the lambing season? I've never been to a sheep farm myself, but I've heard from other Collies that when every ewe is lambing the dogs and humans are working every single hour of the day and night for weeks on end. The humans in the city don't understand any of this. They can't see the farm and what it does because for them, lamb is just something they buy in a shop. It's the same now for you. You can't see that the skills you learned on the farm might be valuable to some humans in the city. There are people here in London who would love to see Collies like you working, because it makes them dream of an easier life, a little place in the country. They don't know about all the hard work that goes on in every farm, but they don't really need to. What you need to understand is that most of the city folk are short of time. They would love to see Collies herding sheep because it takes them away from the city, but they don't have any time to really leave the city and go to watch Collies working on a real farm."

"Do you think it's something that we could do if we get away from here? I mean, do you really think that humans in London would want to watch us doing what we used to do every day on the farm? Where would we find some sheep?"

"I don't have all the answers for you Winston, but what I am saying is that you need to look inside yourself and think about what it is you are really good at. You need a new career, a new purpose. Take a fresh look at your environment, all the space around you. Isn't there some way of being able to get the food and shelter you need just by doing the thing you love?"

Matilda went on: "You know what I do when I want to figure something out or work out my next step? I *paws for thought*. Just stop, take a look around and *paws for thought* without anything disturbing you. Sometimes the way forward is obvious, though sometimes it needs more thought, but if you never stop to think then it will never happen!"

Winston was reenergised. He explained everything to Charlie and Blair, who became even more excited. Blair was so excited he bit the gloves off a young child who had ventured into their kennel. He chewed the gloves. The humans left them alone, upset and without taking a happy dog home.

The next morning, when all the dogs went out for their exercise, Winston could not see

Matilda. She was not on the walk today. He checked her kennel when the dogs all returned back to the home, but she was not there either. She was gone.

Chapter **Five**

Losing Matilda was the final straw. All the other dogs around the Collie's kennel had been out walking as well. None of them had seen anything, so they all assumed the worst. Matilda had ended up in the hands of the doctor, never to return. It was too upsetting for Winston to think about and he resolved that they must all escape together as soon as they possibly could.

The next morning after Matilda vanished, Winston explained his idea to the others: "I'm sure you have noticed how these walkers only ever hold three or four dogs each. I want us to really try today to get one walker to ourselves. I want today to be the day we break free of this place and I'd rather not have any extra baggage."

They agreed. When a sullen-looking Bichon Frise ended up being collected as a part of their group, the three Collies plus the frizz-ball, Blair did his best menacing growl. He pretended it was a stubborn ewe and gave the little dog such a hard time that it whimpered away and begged to be walked by another one of the volunteer walkers.

That was it. They had a walker to themselves and they played along as normal for most of the walk. The walkers usually took them on a circuit that was partially on Battersea Park, but mainly on the streets around the home. Winston had decided that their best chance of escape was to run away from the walker during the walk on the park, because it would be easier to find cover and with dozens of other dogs around on the park all running free, who would notice a few extra?

They got to the park. The sun was shining and it was a warm morning. There were a lot of other dogs running around and playing with their 'normal' owners. These were all dogs that went home to a city house or apartment after their walk, not back to a concrete kennel.

When they caught sight of the lake in Battersea Park their walker stopped for a moment. Her shoelace was loose and she stooped over to check it. She kneeled down and started tying it. Her grip on the three leads had been relaxed so she could use both hands properly to tie up the shoelace. "Run!" called Winston. Charlie and Blair didn't need any more encouragement. They leapt into the freedom of the city park and ran, following Winston's lead. The walker cried out behind them, but within a minute they could no longer hear or see her. Collies can run like the wind, especially when they need to.

Matilda had always advised Winston that if they ever got away, they should head north. Just keep on heading north and forward and don't look back – don't even *paws for thought!* It would allow the dogs to cross several parks, where they could easily mix with other dogs and humans, along with finding food on the way. Matilda had told Winston that even in London, there were plenty of parks. That was good. Surely they would be able to hide in one of the London parks.

So they ran together. The three Collies ran at a breakneck pace through the streets of Chelsea. They stopped and hid together in a small alleyway off Sloane Street. It was partly to catch some breath after the excitement of the escape, but also because Winston wanted to remove the leads they were all dragging. It slowed them down and it also made them look like escapees. They each helped the other to chew through the fabric collars they were wearing. Winston chewed Blair's collar and Blair chewed Charlie's collar and Charlie chewed Winston's collar.

They ran on without collars and quickly found Hyde Park. They were lost in the tunnels beneath Marble Arch, but soon found their way up into Oxford street and so on they ran, always heading north as Matilda had told them to. They found Regent's park and stopped again to rest by the lake. Blair started stalking a Mallard duck and was about to pounce when Winston stopped him: "Cut it out Blair, we don't need to eat just yet. Let's get further north before we worry about food, and anyway there are too many humans around here to start hunting. It's not like the farm."

The Collies ran straight up, and then down, Primrose Hill. They continued on their journey through a patchwork of streets until they found another wooded area. This time it was Hampstead Heath and they managed to continue running, stopping only to bark in wonder at the strange looking ring-necked parakeets on Parliament Hill. They ran on and straight across Highgate golf course before finding themselves in Cherry Tree wood. Now Blair really started complaining – he was in pain. Blair had cut one of his paws on a broken bottle left on a street near the East Finchley tube station. It was bleeding quite badly and he found it difficult to keep running.

Winston reassured Blair, and Charlie: "We just need to go a little further. I think we've gone far enough to get away from the humans at the dog's home, but this wood isn't large enough for us to hide out. Let's just continue until we find somewhere with more space. Not much further now..."

They were lucky. They had started walking after Blair cut his paw, but within ten minutes they found themselves hidden away inside Alexandra Park. After finding a hole in the boundary fence they entered an old cemetery – it was ideal. A huge wooded space with hardly any (living) humans around and wildlife everywhere. The Collies built a small den behind a huge stone memorial marked on the front only with some strange letters – 'BOND'. They rested there and their hopes were raised when Blair's paw took only a few days to heal.

This was truly a great place to live. Winston never failed to remind his friends of what a fine place he had chosen to make their new home. There was water on tap because the humans filled huge vats of water so they could water flowers before putting them on graves and watching them die. There was an unlimited supply of food such as squirrels, rabbits, and muntjacs. The muntjacs were particularly tasty, but quite hard to catch, as their hearing was superb. The den by the stone memorial offered protection from the weather and so they now found that they had shelter, food, and water – and each other. No longer was there any fear for their present or future, but something was missing and Winston knew it. They had no work, no purpose; everything was now just a little too easy. The Collies had left behind a life of imprisonment and entered a life of leisure with no steps in between, and no real effort. To think of their new circumstances sometimes made Winston nauseous. He knew it was better than a constant fear of being taken to the doctor, but he could still not place his paw on the reason for this ennui.

"Never has so much been owed by so many to so few." Winston growled to himself one sunny evening. Matilda had helped them to escape and yet she could not escape from the doctor herself.

"As we now sit in our new-found splendour, Matilda is probably buried beneath a pile of human rubbish – unremembered and unloved."

"Hey! Come quickly! Look what they are doing!" It was Blair charging back into the den and rousing Winston from his brooding and Charlie from his sleep.

"What is it? Are you mad?" Charlie wasn't happy. He had been dreaming about catching grey squirrels. That he had already caught two that same morning didn't stop him dreaming about catching more. Charlie always thought that you can't get too much food, or too many squirrels – they are only tree rats anyway.

"Follow me, I want to show you both something in the field." Blair started leading the others to the fence that acted as a boundary between the cemetery and a long line of football pitches. The Collies never really crossed into the football pitches. They had no reason to leave the cemetery and there was nothing for them that they could need in a football pitch anyway.

But when they arrived at the boundary fence this time the Collies could see there was a group of humans with dogs of all different shapes and sizes all out there on the field, trying to do something, led by one human who was clearly the leader. They were trying to herd! But they weren't herding sheep, the leader had a goose and he was asking the dogs to herd it back into a wooden pen. They were right here in the city herding a goose!

Winston, Charlie, and Blair watched transfixed. The city dogs were useless. Some of them even attacked the goose and had to be taken away by their shameful owners.

"Just look at them! They can't even herd a single goose!" Blair was crying out to the others as they watched. "Remember how the three of us together could manage a field of hundreds of sheep, and these city dogs can't even direct a single goose?"

Winston watched, and watched. He wanted to find a way of taking part and showing the skills he knew he and his friends possessed, but he could not find a way through the fence.

They also had no owner, so there was no way to easily approach the group. But what had really caught his attention was a Staffordshire bull terrier, one of the dogs that tried to eat the goose rather than herding it. The owner had taken the dog away from the group, but the owner had not scolded the dog, merely told it to try harder next week. That Staffie looked very familiar.

Chapter **Six**

The Collies returned each day to the boundary fence to watch and see if the humans and dogs returned again with the geese. They didn't come for six days, but then on the seventh day – at about the same time – Blair spotted the leader there on the field all alone. He ran back to the den to call the other Collies.

"I should have guessed they would only be meeting once a week. It must be a local dog club for people living here in the city. I think it's Monday today, so they must get together every Monday to try training their dogs." Winston was talking, but it was as if he was muttering to himself. Winston had not even considered that there might be a weekly class for people who need to train their dogs. It was something you had to learn on the farm just to live together, but now he realised that it was obvious. This was the city. People don't have any time.

Charlie said: "Hang on a moment Winston, keep the noise down. Look, the leader is out there training his own dog with the goose again, and his dog looks a bit like a Collie."

Winston was not sure what to do next. It would be easier to approach the leader and his dog, rather than to try approaching a group of twenty dogs, all with their owners wondering who these rough-looking Collies might be. Before he could think further though, Charlie and Winston spotted Blair running up to the leader and his dog.

Blair was right in front of them both. He stopped and said: "Hello. I'm Blair. Who are you? What are you doing out here?"

The almost-Collie smiled and answered right away. He seemed very friendly and not at all how the Collies expected a city dog to behave: "I'm Elvis. It's nice to meet you. Are you from around here? I know I look a bit like a Collie, but I'm actually a cross between a Lurcher and a Collie and I think that there was some Irish Wolfhound a few generations back because I love a drop of Guinness on Sundays. It means I've got a bit of the herding instinct in me, but also the speed of a greyhound and fantastic sight. Are you a pure Collie then?"

Blair said: "Yes, I'm a pure Collie. I'm from a farm outside of London, but my friends and me have been living close to here. We used to herd sheep everyday. I saw you herding the goose. Can I have a go?"

Elvis barked at his owner. The man looked at Elvis and Blair together and smiled. He had already set up the wooden pen for the goose, so he just took the crate he was holding the bird in and opened it up.

"Go on then, let's see you work" called Elvis as the goose flapped across the field, running about as fast as a fat bird can run.

Blair wasted no time. He hadn't forgotten a thing. He looped around in a huge sweeping arc to the left-hand side of the goose. He then crept up directly on the goose as it continued running. The bird was shocked to find a dog right in its path and immediately turned one hundred and eighty degrees, spinning around and running back to the man and his almost-Collie. Blair guided the goose straight into the pen without the goose making any further protest.

Elvis was impressed: "You really are good. Are your friends around as well?"

Blair called out to Winston and Charlie. They ran a bit faster when they saw that the man was rewarding Blair with pieces of sausage. The man carried on releasing the goose and letting each of the dogs herd it back to the pen. Winston and Charlie could get the goose back into the pen even faster than Blair. Winston hardly even had to move, he just looked at the goose and it gave up and walked into the pen. Elvis's owner ended up laughing out loud: "You boys are the finest herders I have ever seen. I come here each week training these people and their dogs. Some of them are at it for years and they still can't get it right!"

The man introduced himself to the dogs as "Uncle John. You can call me Uncle John, and if you don't have a home to go to then you are more than welcome to come back to my home with Elvis. I'd like to put you through your paces and to have a go at some trials if you would like it. I've got plenty of good food at home as well. And it's about time all of you had a bath!"

Uncle John led his class that evening, calling on Winston, Charlie, and Blair to give examples to the others. He was praising them all evening, calling them 'wonder dogs', calling them a 'credit to their breed', and saying that 'all your pets need to learn from dogs like this'. Winston, Charlie, and Blair were beaming with pride, and they found that the city dogs actually welcomed them. Elvis was great. He was a real Collie, just with a bit of Lurcher and Guinness mixed in as well. He loved learning new tricks from the Collies. The city dogs relished the chance to learn about how best to control the goose. There were a few boneheads amongst the class. Some of them could not understand that if they got the goose in the pen, they would get some sausage. They just tried to eat the goose, but there are always a few dunces in every class. Most of the dogs treated the Collies as if they were visiting experts from a faraway place. They were visiting professors of the canine world.

Winston's vision had not failed him the previous week. One owner arrived late for the class and was apologising, with her little brindle Staffordshire bull terrier sitting and wagging its tail – waiting to start the session. Winston called out: "Matilda? Is that you?"

The Staffie responded: "Winston? Charlie, Blair – how on earth did you get here? You escaped?"

"Yes, we finally escaped and ran north – just as you said. We thought you were gone."

"I was picked out by a new owner who lives around here. They came to the dog's home very early one day and I never had a chance to say goodbye to anyone. I had no idea I was leaving until they packed me into the back of a car. I go for walks here everyday now. We live just on the other side of the wood. It's great here!"

Winston was beaming. He had found his old friend from the dog's home once again. He also loved the attention from the class. He looked up at Uncle John once, as Charlie was leading a West Highland Terrier through the best way to capture the goose once it tries making a break for freedom. Uncle John patted his head and said "That'll do boy"... so was this the pleasure they might get in finding an owner in the city or would they need to remain in the cemetery? The question was answered later that evening once the class had dispersed.

They stayed with Elvis and Uncle John as he cleared up. Eventually the two of them were ready to go. As Uncle John climbed into his car, a large jeep with lots of space for dogs in the back, he called to the Collies: "Come on then!"

All three of the Collies leaped into the car and joined Elvis in the back. They returned to Uncle John's house where he introduced the new dogs to his wife. She fed them all biscuits and cleared a space for them to sleep on soft blankets. Elvis thought it was great to have some new friends around the house. Matilda had given details of the times she would normally be out in the woods, so they would know when to look out for her again.

Uncle John was talking to his wife over dinner: "You know what, these dogs are the best herding animals I have ever seen. Absolute masters. They must have come from a farm originally – they couldn't have learned that in the city. I'm going to start taking them to some country shows, maybe a few trials, and maybe even some corporate work where companies want to do something different. They really know how to work as a team and I'm going to show them to the world..." Uncle John was smiling. It looked as if he was as pleased to find the dogs as they were to find him.

Winston looked at Charlie and Blair and smiled. The three Collies were sprawled together on their blanket in a safe and warm new home full of biscuits and snacks. He said to the other Collies: "Matilda always said she didn't have any answers, but she predicted our future. We worked hard, looked outside our usual environment and now we've found that our skills really are valued in a place where we never imagined they would be. All we ever really needed to do was *paws for thought*. If we had done that earlier, we would have seen how vulnerable our old jobs on the farm really were."

Blair replied: "Yes Winston. Our old jobs moved but we found new ones – and this house is a lot nicer than the old barn. Give me a couch and soft blanket over a handful of straw any day!"

Winston laughed and said: "We have our family, shelter, and food and we are doing the thing we love most. We truly are the luckiest dogs alive today and it's all thanks to the farmer."

Then Winston's face changed. He became serious, as if a cloud had suddenly floated across his field of vision. He said to the others: "You know when the farmer introduced the other dogs and we trained them, I didn't believe what was happening. I couldn't understand that anything was changing. Then, when it was too late and we were already at the dog's home, I was afraid and eventually angry. How could he desert us after all our hard work? Then, as we started meeting new people, like Matilda, it seemed that there could be a life away from the farm and that it may even be fun. Once we managed to flee the dog's home and found our new home at the BOND, I started accepting that even the things you are scared of can sometimes be better than the things you know. Do you think life is always like that when something big changes the way you see the world?"

But Charlie was already asleep; Blair was almost sleeping too and he only grunted an acknowledgement. Winston was getting too philosophical for the others, who were tired from a day of working with Uncle John.

Winston said goodnight to Elvis and also drifted off, dreaming all the time about herding sheep, but not down on the farm – now his dreams featured nothing more than herding in the park.

Afterword and **Final Thoughts**

Winston, Charlie, and Blair managed to find a new job even after the farmer found a new way to resource his farm. They found a new purpose and new goals by opening their eyes to possibilities they had not seen before. This is something we can all do. It's becoming something we all need to do.

This is an issue that affects us all – not just Collies trying to find a new career away from the farm. As it becomes more common to source services from remote global locations, what is possible to deliver remotely expands in scope. Companies are now exploring all kinds of services that could never be remotely delivered in the past; accounting, human resources, research, editing, legal analysis... the world is changing fast and both you and I need to adapt to that change if we want a job next year.

Migration is also increasing as people become more willing to search out the best opportunities and legislators create visa programmes designed to fill skills gaps. The European Union allows a free movement of labour within the union, but specific government plans often use a points system to decide if someone is an attractive migrant or not. In short, if you have some good work experience and a few qualifications then it is likely you can work almost anywhere you can find a job.

When my granddad John came to England seeking work, most locals generally hated the Irish. Landlords would post notices on their doors stating 'No Blacks, No Dogs, No Irish' – maybe in varying order as they were all seen as approximately the same level of degenerate back then. The USA has worried for years about Mexican immigration. Western Europe is presently worried about the migrants from Eastern Europe, particularly Poland. Although the populist view on migration is often negative and reflects a feeling that 'foreigners come here to work for less and steal our jobs' the reality is that over this century most developed nations are going to see an extreme demographic change. The proportion of retired citizens will increase dramatically and the number of active citizens working and contributing income tax will reduce. By the middle of this century it is estimated that fewer than half of all Germans will be economically active. The majority will be either elderly or children, neither contributing to government finances. So how can a developed country like Germany continue to expect economic growth at the same time as maintaining the existing social welfare standards – all with fewer people working and contributing to the economic welfare of the nation? Some migration will be essential and some offshoring of tasks will be essential if countries faced with these challenges are to remain competitive and economically relevant in the twenty-first century.

As demonstrated by the modern USA, migration can shape a nation and benefit the economy and social fabric of society. In my own country, the United Kingdom, our most popular food came from India, and some of our best sporting heroes were born in various locations across the Commonwealth.

The debate on offshoring and migration needs to be considered within the context of how work itself is changing. Just as the Border Collies in this story found, there is always an alternate future, though it may not be obvious. Remember when the career you trained for, and possibly went to university to study for, would remain unchanged for a lifetime? Now it can only be taken as read that many skills learned in one decade are outdated in the next. A university degree is no longer a one-way ticket to career success.

Those of us in mature societies need to consider how deeply our expectations of society may need to change. Our systems of education, social security, and income tax may need to be scrapped and rebuilt. Our ideas that the state itself may entirely support pension age citizens will almost certainly need to be scrapped. I'm still in my 30s and my country provides a state pension. By the time I retire, I expect it will be down to every man and woman alone to sort out his or her own affairs; or at best the state pension will exist, but be at such a low level it is impossible to live on. Our concept of schooling and education will need to be rebuilt along a need to undergo life-long education – not education we can opt out of at sixteen.

But there are new opportunities too. The deep expertise developed in countries such as Germany means that it is their machinery Indian and Chinese manufacturers turn to when they want the best. Companies the world over still come to London or New York when they want to raise capital from issuing public shares. Expertise and experience remains important because value is always measured differently to cost.

Predicting the future is impossible, but there is one certainty. This is going to be an Asian century. To the Chinese, China is just making a comeback and India is not far behind. Europe and the USA can co-exist with the rapidly developing Asian nations, but we can't assume that things are going to be just the way they always were through the nineteenth and twentieth centuries – the era of Occidental hegemony. Anyone who does will soon be asking an important question:

'Who moved my job?'

Our Community

For more information about this book and the author, why not come and visit the 'Who Moved My Job?' online community? Here you can read messages from Mark, discuss your thoughts about the book, and interact with other readers. There's no need to *paws for thought* – just head to this website:

www.whomovedmyjob.com